READING POWER

EXTREME SPORTS™

Skateboarding
CHECK IT OUT!

Kristin Eck

The Rosen Publishing Group's
PowerKids Press™
New York

SAFETY GEAR, INCLUDING HELMETS, KNEE PADS, WRIST PADS, AND ELBOW PADS SHOULD BE WORN WHILE SKATEBOARDING. DO NOT ATTEMPT TRICKS WITHOUT PROPER GEAR, INSTRUCTION, AND SUPERVISION.

For Mike

Published in 2001 by The Rosen Publishing Group, Inc.
29 East 21st Street, New York, NY 10010

First Edition

Book Design: Michael de Guzman
Layout: Felicity Erwin, Nick Sciacca

Photo Credits: p. 5 © Jamie Squire/Allsport; p. 7 © Ben Liversedge; pp. 9, 13, 17 © Thaddeus Harden; p. 11 © Hank deVre/Mountain Stock; pp. 14, 19 © Tony Donaldson.

Eck, Kristin.
    Skateboarding / Kristin Eck.— 1st ed.
        p. cm. — (Reading power) (Extreme sports)
    Includes bibliographical references and index.
    Summary: Simple text describes the parts of a skateboard, other skateboarding equipment, and skateboarding stunts.
    ISBN 0-8239-5695-4 (alk. paper)
    1. Skateboarding—Juvenile literature. [1. Skateboarding.] I. Title. II. Series. III.Series: Extreme sports
    GV859.8 . E35 2001
    796.22—dc21   00-020168

Manufactured in the United States of America

2

Contents

Lots of people like to skateboard. Friends can skateboard together.

Mothers and daughters can skateboard together.

A skateboarder needs a skateboard. A skateboarder needs knee pads and elbow pads. A skateboarder needs a helmet, too.

9

Skateboards can be different colors. You can pick the color you like.

You can skateboard on
the ground.

13

You can skateboard in the air.

Tony Hawk can jump high with his skateboard. Tony Hawk has skateboarded for a long time. He is a skateboarding champion.

17

The ollie is a skateboarding move. You go up in the air. The skateboard goes up in the air, too.

Skating on a rail is a hard trick. This skateboarder wears his helmet. Good skateboarders are safe skateboarders!

21

Glossary

champion (CHAM-pee-un) The best, or the winner.

elbow pads (EL-boh PADS) Pads with a hard plastic shell worn to protect the elbows.

helmet (HEL-mit) What skateboarders wear to keep their heads safe.

knee pads (NEE PADS) Pads with a hard plastic shell worn to protect the knees.

ollie (AH-lee) A special skateboarding move, or trick, where the rider and the board lift off the ground.

rail (RAYL) A horizontal (side-to-side) bar supported by vertical (up-and-down) posts.

together (too-GEH-thur) With another person, or other people.

trick (TRIHK) A special, or difficult, move or stunt.

Here are more books to read about
skateboarding:

Skateboarding Basics
(New Action Sports)
by Jackson Jay
Capstone Press (1996)

Skateboarding
(Adventurers)
by Jeremy Evans
and Graham Morecroft
Crestwood House (1994)

To learn more about skateboarding,
check out this Web site:

http://www.skateboarding.com

Index

Word Count: 118

Note to Librarians, Teachers, and Parents

If reading is a challenge, Reading Power is a solution! Reading Power is perfect for readers who want high-interest subject matter at an accessible reading level. These fact-filled, photo-illustrated books are designed for readers who want straightforward vocabulary, engaging topics, and a manageable reading experience. With clear picture/text correspondence, leveled Reading Power books put the reader in charge. Now readers have the power to get the information they want and the skills they need in a user-friendly format.